Best wishes from
Bob & Delphine Mutchler

3/23/85

Lene Mayer-Skumanz

The Story of
Brother Francis

Art by Alicia Sancha

Translated from the German by Hildegard Bomer

The Story of Brother Francis has won the Austrian
Children's Book Prize from that country's Ministry of
Education and Art, and the Catholic Children's Book
Prize, awarded by the German Conference of Bishops.

AVE MARIA PRESS   Notre Dame, Indiana

On the slope of a green hill in Italy
there is a small town
with narrow streets
as crooked as the backs of angry cats.
The tiled roofs shine red
on houses of light-colored stone,
each with a garden
and flower boxes under the windows.
Its name is Assisi.
Over seven hundred years ago,
there lived here
a little boy with dark hair and merry eyes.
His name was Francis Bernadone.

"Little Francis is a real rascal," said the people.
"No fruit tree, no vineyard is safe.
He's even started a gang
that plays soldiers and robbers,
and screams and fights."
"My Francis is not bad, only lively," said his mother.
"He got that from me," said his father proudly.
And they spoiled him very much.

His father was a wealthy merchant
who sold the most beautiful cloth
in the whole region:
silk and velvet, fancy lace,
wool the color of blue grapes,
silver-green olives and red carnations.
Little Francis liked the colorful fabrics.
His father said: "Francis,
one day you will be better off than I am.
You will be even wealthier and more powerful."

He gave Francis a red jacket,
a neat cap and fine boots,
the finest in all Assisi.

The next day Francis had no cap,
and the day after that he had no boots.
"Francis, where is your cap?" asked his father.
"Where are your boots?"
"Gone," said Francis.
"Be more careful with your things!" said his father.
"One does not lose fine boots and a new cap!"
"I did not lose them," said Francis. "I gave them away."
"But to whom?" asked his father.
"To my friends," said Francis.
"Peter had no cap and Paul had no shoes."
"But Francis!" cried his father. "Fine things cost money.
I don't earn money so that you can give your things to your friends.
Remember: a good merchant does not give things away!"

"I don't know if I want to be a merchant," said Francis.
"I think I'll be a knight."

Francis and his young friends
all wanted to become knights.
So they made their own swords, shields and helmets;
they decorated their helmets with grass and rooster feathers.
They carved bows and arrows.
With Francis as their leader
they went in search of adventure:
adventure with strange dogs,
adventure with boys of neighboring towns.
Every evening they came home, tired and dirty.
Every evening after his mother had bathed him,
Francis begged, "Tell me a story!"

His mother told him tales and legends about
giants and robbers,
dragons and magicians,
fairies and knights—
over and over again about knights.

"Knights are good and kind to all people," said his mother.
"Knights are brave, loyal and obedient to their king.
They protect the poor, the sick and the weak
and spare the enemy when he asks for mercy.
Remember, Francis, a knight is good to everybody!"
"Even to the bad boys of the neighbors?" asked Francis.
"Even to them!" said his mother.
"Even to the birds and their babies in the nest?"
"Of course, Francis, even to the birds."
"Even to the earthworms, Mother?"
"But why not?"
"Then I must be kind to the fishes and flowers, too,"
said Francis. "Otherwise it would not be fair."
"Then go and be kind to every living and growing thing which
God has created," said his mother.

Francis could whistle and sing loudly.
He could run almost as fast as the wind.
He ran the fastest if one of his friends called him.
Then he even ran away from his dinner.
"Stop, Francis, eat your soup first!" his mother would call.
But Francis would already be down the stairs.

"This won't do," said his mother in the evening.
"To run away from dinner is not at all polite."
But then Francis would talk and talk,
and explain
why it was so important for him to run away.
"I cannot leave my friends alone
when they need me!
Mother, don't you understand that?"
"Oh, Francis, you are talking with your hands and feet!"
said his mother.
"Can't you sit still for just five minutes?"

Francis usually could *not* sit still for more than five minutes.
But he would sit very still when he watched the crested lark.
Crested larks are brown like the earth,
and have a funny crown of feathers.
They fly high in the blue sky
and sing their songs of joy.

He would also sit quietly when he watched the sun,
soaking up the warmth of the shining disk,
brilliant and beautiful
and mysterious in its fire.

Francis would sit very quietly and observe the water
as it ran clear and fresh to the fountain,
as it sprayed the flowers and grass
with glittering drops.
And Francis saw how the drops
rolled down the leaves,
hung to the edges and fell to the ground.

Francis sat very quietly when his mother sang him songs:
songs for laughing,
songs for sighing,
songs for dreaming.
"I don't know if I want to be a knight," said little Francis.
"I think I'll become a singer.
Being a singer I'll wander through the whole country
and make up songs.

A funny song for someone who cries,
a gentle song for someone who is angry,
a brave song for someone who is afraid.
A song for the mosquitoes,
a song for rabbits,
a song for the fish in the water."
"Fish don't listen to singers," said his mother.
"Oh," said Francis, "maybe nobody has tried it yet,
and the fish are still waiting."

His friends always thought Francis had the best ideas,
even when they all grew up and became real knights.
Now their helmets were decorated with gold and silver
and their swords had sharp cutting edges.
Francis was the leader as always,
and their feasts were loud and wild,
much too loud for the small town with the small gardens.
When the moon shone over the mountains
the young people sang as they wandered
through the crooked narrow streets of Assisi.
They awakened the girls,
the fathers and mothers,
the servants and maids
and the dogs, cats and chickens.

There was much laughing
and scolding and barking
and cackling and mewing
in the town.
"Of course, it's Francis," said the people.
"He thinks he can do as he pleases."

"My son is just fine, let him have a fling," said his father.
"My son is not wild, just a lot of fun," said his mother.
"I am glad that he is happy and healthy in these hard times."

Those were times of war and strife in the whole country.
One town fought against another,
each wanted to be more powerful than its neighbors.
Even the small town of Assisi had its own soldiers.
"Finally we can be heroes!"
cried Francis and his friends
as they went to war.

But they were caught and imprisoned
and their families had to pay a great ransom
to free them.
When Francis came home,
he was not happy and healthy.
For a long time he stayed in bed with a fever.
"If I only could get up again," he thought.
"If I only could ride and sing
and make merry again!"

But when he could get up
his old pastimes gave him no pleasure.
The banquets were too long,
the songs too boring,
his friends too loud.
Francis was surprised. "What is the matter with me?"

"You only need some fresh air!" said his mother.
"Go ride your horse a bit!"
Francis saddled his horse
and rode through the vineyards down to the plain.

Far from the walls of the city
in the shadow of some chestnut trees
was the hospital where the lepers lived.
They were not allowed to enter the city
because their disease was so awful
that it could not be cured.
The sick got ugly sores all over their bodies,
then the sores would break, and bleed and stink—
hands and feet rotted away on some lepers
and some became blind.
They lived together
and helped one another as well as they could.
Those who could still walk led the blind.
Those who still had hands
fed those who didn't.

Francis had always sent money and food to the sick.
He felt sorry for them,
but he had yet to visit them.
If he rode past the hospital
he would hold his nose
and turn his head away.
It made him sick to see all this suffering.

But this time he paid no attention to where he was riding.
Suddenly he heard a yell.
He lifted his head and saw it:
there was the hospital.
In front of the door
sat a sick man begging—
"Have pity, young man, give me something!"

Francis threw his moneybag to the man.
The purse fell into the dust in front of the sick man.
"Thank you!" he cried. "You're a kind young man!
May God reward you a thousand times!"
He stretched out to pick up the purse.
But he could not reach it.
Then he crawled
with much effort
on his rotted legs.
Francis saw that the man had no feet.

"Wait!" cried Francis.
He climbed from his horse,
and ran to pick up the moneybag.
"Forgive me!" he said.
He put the purse into the man's hand.

"Don't touch me!" called out the sick man.
"You might catch this sickness."
But Francis had already held the man's hand—
a pitiful hand with bleeding fingers.
He looked down at it and said: "This must be bandaged!"
"I have no water and I have no bandages," said the man.
"God help you!" cried Francis.
"Tomorrow," he promised,
"I will come again and bring bandages and water
and help you bandage your wounds."

With healthy legs Francis mounted his horse,
and with healthy hands took the reins.
He wore soft, beautiful clothes,
feathers on his hat,
and his boots were surely the finest in Assisi.

In front of the poor sick man Francis felt ashamed.
He laid his head on the neck of his horse and cried.
He cried so much that
the mane and the blanket
were wet from his tears.
The horse knew its way,
and took its master home.

"I am afraid of the hospital," thought Francis,
"afraid of the wounds and of the stench."
But he loaded blankets, bandages and food on his horse
and went to the hospital.
He worked for the sick all day long.
When he climbed to the woods in the evening he was tired.
There he found a small chapel, its door slightly open;
he entered, sat on a rickety wooden bench
and rested.
It was dark and quiet,
with no light in front of the cross.
But Francis could still see Jesus
in the shadows on the cross.
He looked and wondered who was to be pitied more,
those in the hospital without hands and feet
or the man on the cross,
whose hands and feet were pierced by nails.
And Francis remembered what Jesus had said:
"What you do unto the least of my brethren,
you do unto me."

"Well, then," said Francis to Jesus on the cross,
"I have gotten to know you a little today.
I carried water for you and I bathed you.
You let it happen and were not ashamed before me.
I have bandaged your wounds, anxiously and awkwardly,
and you thanked me in spite of your hurt.
I warmed soup for you and fed you bit by bit,
and you ate obediently like a child with his mother.
Then you had enough and you asked me
to tell you something about life outside,
about the town and its people.
I told you and sang the new songs,
the way the minstrels sing them,
and you asked: 'Will you come again?'
And I promised that I would,
and I will get to know you, Jesus, a bit more tomorrow!"

His mother was happy
when she heard Francis
play the lute that evening in his room.
"Finally," she said, "something is giving him pleasure again!"

But his friends were not happy with Francis anymore.
"He's a bit crazy!
Hospital and woods,
woods and hospital,
he doesn't know anything else."

"Francis, come with us," they yelled.
"We need you for our banquet!
Hey, Francis, are you deaf?
Don't you hear when we call you?"
Francis waved to them.
"I hear," he said. "But my sick friends
call louder than you!"
"They call? We can't hear it!" said his friends.
"Your ears apparently have become very sharp lately."

They laughed at him, but Francis was not hurt.
He thought: "It is true, what they say.
My ears have become sharp.
I am called from everywhere.
The woods call me,
the quiet calls,
the cave is calling me.
I am called by the poor people, by the animals,
and I am called by Jesus on the cross."

He went to the chapel in the woods, where he knelt down and said:
"Here I am! I want to be your servant.
I would like to know you so well
that I will know for sure what I should do for you.
And when I know it, I want to do it—
if you will help me!
Because I can't do it alone!"

Everything Francis did these days displeased his father.
"Francis, you fool!" cried his father.
"Come here! I must speak with you!
Look at you! You look like a mason!
Your clothes are full of mortar!"

"The little chapel of San Damiano is falling apart,"
answered Francis. "I am rebuilding it!"

"Are you a poor servant or a rich merchant?" asked his father.
"Yesterday you sold our most expensive cloth.
Where is the money?"

"I still have it," said Francis.
"I would like to give it to the poor."
"Are you crazy?" asked his father. "What are we earning money for?
To give it away?"
Francis handed the money to his father.
"Father, the money does not belong to us. We have enough to live on.
We owe the money to those who have less than we do!"

"What silly ideas are these?" cried his father.
He hit Francis and made him stay at home.
But Francis did not stop speaking about the poor.
Finally his father took Francis to visit the bishop.
"Bishop," he complained, "my son Francis,
to whom I have given everything,
life and home, food and drink,
clothing, hats and boots,
does not want to obey me anymore!"

So Francis took off his clothes
and gave them back to his father.
He stood there naked and cried out:
"Now I have only my father in heaven!
I will obey him gladly, for he lets me be poor,
poor like his son Jesus."

The bishop's gardener gave Francis an old coat.
And so he left Assisi—in his old coat.
He went to the hospital and asked: "May I live here?"

The sick people were horrified,
when they heard
that Francis had given up everything.
"Are you no longer the rich merchant's heir?
How can you help us, if you are as poor as we are?"
"Don't be afraid, my friends!" said Francis.
"I will go and beg for you!"

Francis then went begging from door to door
asking for food and bandages for the lepers,
for mortar and stones for the chapel.
People made fun of him.
Boys ran after him,
threw dirt and stones at him,
yelling: "The woodsman! The fool!"

Francis was not angry.
He sang at the market
for people who wanted to listen;
he sang songs about the good Lord
who gives peace to mankind.

Francis helped the peasants in the fields,
and the shepherds
guarding their sheep.
He begged from his old friends,
but they did not understand him.
"What is so beautiful about being poor?
You're pitiful, Francis."
He answered:
"Yes I am, but I am blessed to be poor!
I do not have to guard my money.
I am not afraid of thieves and robbers.
I do not need a sword.
I am not anxious about tomorrow,
because tomorrow I will be as poor as today.
I am free, because I want to be poor."

"It's a shame about Francis," said his friends.
"He really is crazy!"
"My Francis is not crazy, only very good," said his mother.
"My little knight has found his king.
Jesus was poor. Should his messenger be rich?
Jesus loved mankind and died for us.
What other song should a minstrel sing?"

When a man gives away
all he owns, for the love of God,
every hour he finds
God's gifts to him.
God gave Francis a shady tree
next to a dusty street
so that he could rest after a walk.
And Francis knew this was a gift.
God gave Francis a cave in the woods
for thinking, sleeping and praying in.
And Francis knew this was a gift.
God gave Francis
the sun, the moon, and the stars,
fresh rain from the sky,
cool winds from the mountains,
clear water from the stream,
grapes, flowers, olives,
even beautiful stones,
and Francis understood and was amazed: so many gifts!

God also gave Francis friends—
animals and people.
When a cricket
jumped on his hand
he coaxed it
and it sang for him.

When a fish was caught in the net
Francis set him free
and wished him well;
and the fish swam around the boat
in friendly circles
and jumped out of the lake
so that the water drops shimmered.
Even the wild wolf with green eyes
became gentle
when Francis called him brother.

Then other young men from the town
gave all their money to the poor and said:
"Francis, now we are as poor as you.
Can't you use brothers to help you
take care of the sick
and sing and be happy with you?"
Francis was very glad.
They built small cottages
around a little, poor church outside of town.
The church was called Portiuncula, just as it is today.

Francis and his new brothers
helped anybody who needed them—
in the house, in the stable
baking bread,
weaving baskets
or washing.
No work was too hard for them.
They took no wages, only a handful of food.
They wanted to be the poorest of the poor
and to show how to live peacefully.
The people in the town and in the villages were astonished.
They said: "They are happier
than we are in our strong houses,
with our trunks full of furs and cloth,
and our tables spread with food.
Who dares still laugh about them?
They bring blessings to our land!"

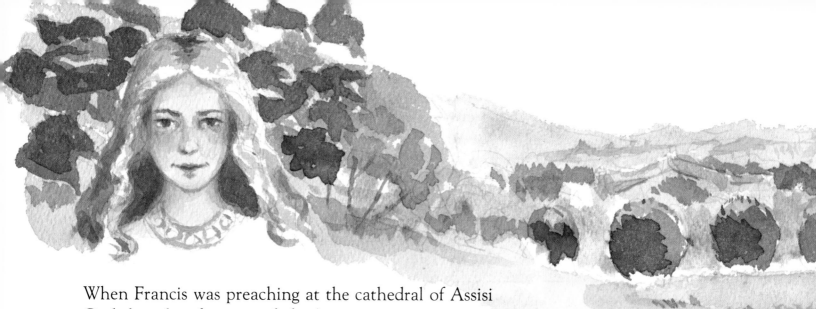

When Francis was preaching at the cathedral of Assisi
God thought of a new gift for him:
Clare.
She was 16 years old
and knew exactly what she wanted.
Like Francis she too followed Jesus.
Secretly she left the home of her wealthy parents
and became a poor sister in a convent.
She lived up on the mountain near San Damiano,
near the chapel in the woods where Brother Francis first
had spoken with Jesus.
"Clare, how can you do this?"
asked her parents, her friends, the maids and the servants.
Clare said:
"Too many people are wealthy,
therefore I want to be poor.
Too many people talk too much,
therefore I want to be silent.
Too many people forget poor Jesus,
therefore I want to think of him."

The brothers wore coarse brown robes with hoods.
Some wandered through the whole land
speaking about God.
Others lived in quiet corners
praising God for his works.
Francis would have preferred to be a hermit,
far away from the noise of the cities,
alone among the trees and rocks
in the presence of God.
But he did not want to decide by himself which was better;
to wander the country preaching
or praising God in solitude.
Francis sent a brother to Clare,
for he had much confidence in her.
And Clare sent her answer back,
"Francis, God has not called you for your sake.
He has called you
that you may remind people of Jesus.
A minstrel does not sing his songs for himself.
He sings them for the pleasure of those who hear him."

When Francis heard that, he got up quickly,
forgot his tired feet and cried:
"Then I want to do the work that has been given to me.
Over and over again.
I will tell people and animals of the good Lord."

He went into the fields
and waved to the crested larks and the swallows,
to the doves and the finches,
and called to them:
"Birds, my brothers,
you should praise and glorify God!
He has given you beautiful voices
wings to fly with
and colorful feathers for your dress!
Mountains and hills, rocks and trees
he has made,
so that you may build nests for your young ones!
He gives you grain from the field
and water from the stream—
can you feel how he loves you?
Be glad and praise him for it!"

And so the birds fluttered their wings
and opened their beaks
to sing and chirp
a happy song of thanksgiving.

"My brothers, the birds, understand me," said Francis.
"I hope that my brothers and sisters
understand me just as well,
here and in other countries,
now and in later times,
on both sides of the sea."

In those times many ships filled with crusaders
crossed the sea
to conquer the Holy Land.
They went forth with spears and swords,
swearing, "All people should have the same faith we have!"
The people on the other side of the ocean believed in Allah
and his prophets
and fought for their faith with fire and sword.

Francis, too, got on a ship and crossed the ocean.
He saw the crusaders storm against the armies of the sultan
and thought: "I must tell all of them about God,
our knights and also the others.
I won't fight with the sword."

Barefoot,
and without weapons,
Francis walked into the sultan's camp and asked:
"Lead me to your master!"

The soldiers hurried to the sultan
with this strange slight man,
the one from the other side,
without sword, and without fear.
"He wants to speak with you!"
"Speak!" said the sultan.
"Sultan!" he began, "God loves us all,
freely and fully.
He does not owe us love.

He gives it to us, his children.
We cannot be greedy with his love,
but must pass it on in peace!"

The sultan thought:
"This small man is not at all like the proud knights
who fight against me.
I can easily conquer those men with swords!
But against one who loves,
one who is gentle?
What weapon can I use against such a man?
There is no weapon against love!
Woe is me! If the knights of the West
fought with love instead of swords,
I would have to surrender!"

And the sultan said to Francis:
"You are unique in the world.
You are favored by God.
I will think about what you say of love and peace—
if one of the commanders from the West
wants to negotiate in peace with me!"

But at that time there was not one
among the knights and kings,
who wanted to negotiate in peace.
They preferred to fight;
and many died.
Francis saw this and he could not help them,
because they would not listen.
And so he went back home to Italy.

Again Francis wandered the cities and villages.
If he met people who were even poorer than he
he happily gave them all he could—
his robe, his last piece of bread, his hood.
"Francis, are you not too hard on yourself?"
asked his brothers and friends.
"You give and give, and you yourself are hungry and cold!"
Francis looked at them and laughed and said:
"I am the eagle who coaxes his young ones to fly."

One day Francis found a rabbit in the field
that was caught in a trap.

He freed the rabbit and petted it.
"Brother rabbit," asked Francis,
"how did you get caught in the trap?
You have to keep your eyes open
and look where you run.
Promise me this and go hop into your woods!"

But the rabbit did not want to leave Francis.
Wherever Francis went he hopped beside him.
"Brother rabbit, this can't go on,"
said Francis as he crouched down beside him.
"Look, I am going to town now
where there are people and dogs,
and all would love to eat a rabbit.
In the woods you have your nest and your family.
So be good and turn around!"

The rabbit hopped slowly across the meadow.
"Hey, brother rabbit!" cried Francis.
"You are so sad, your ears hang down!
A good rabbit should never have sad ears,
because sadness can spread.
Be happy, brother rabbit,
for the sake of the other rabbits!"
The rabbit sat up,
cocked his ears and sniffed the air.
"That's the way!" said Francis.
The rabbit made a sharp turn and ran back to the woods.

Francis had always liked to celebrate.
In the Sabiner mountains
there lived a friend
called Hans.
"Hans," said Francis, "do you know
that cave in the cliff up in the woods?
I would like to celebrate Christmas there with you and our friends.
Take a manger, fill it with hay
and put it up in the cave.
And bring an ox and a donkey!"
On Christmas Eve everything was ready
just the way Francis had wished it.
Peasants and shepherds came from everywhere.
They came up the snowy paths
singing the songs the shepherds sing in the mountains.
They carried torches in their hands,
and the snow was rosy from the dancing flames.

Francis led his friends to the manger.
"Just imagine,
in such a poor manger
once lay the Christ child
and an ox and ass looked at him!
See how poor he was for our sake:
A child who had nothing
and needed
food, warmth, and clothes.
He could not speak and ask: Give me this or that!
He only cried and his mother would guess:
Is my child hungry?
Is something hurting him?
Should I change him?
The son of God became a man like us."
The brothers and shepherds and peasants were moved
and knelt in the snow and said:
"We have never before imagined it so well.
God, your love is so great we cannot comprehend it!"

Even now many people do what Brother Francis did.
They put up a manger at Christmas
with ox and ass and hay and a lantern,
and they sing songs together about the child Jesus.

Two years before he died
Francis had a wonderful experience.
He, who loved Jesus so much
and wanted to be like him,
noticed the wounds of Jesus on his own body.
Only very few friends saw the wounds;
none dared ask questions,
and Francis did not speak about them.
It was a secret between God and himself.
Clare understood this and was silent
but she made
a pair of soft shoes for Francis
out of wool and fur
so that he still could walk
on his poor wounded feet.

Francis became very ill.
For days he lay in Clare's garden at San Damiano.
His eyes hurt and he could not see anymore.
But he had seen enough in his life
and he knew the beauty of everything that God had created.
He called one of his brothers and said:
"I have composed a song.
Write it down, so that all people everywhere can sing it."

Be praised, my Lord,
with all your creatures,
above all else our brother sun,
who brings us day and light.
Beautiful is he
and radiant in his splendor.
His meaning comes from you, most high.

Be praised, my Lord,
for sister moon and the stars.
You have placed them in the heavens,
clear and precious and beautiful.

Be praised, my Lord,
for brother wind and the air
and clouds and blue skies
and every kind of weather,
which you send for the sustenance of your creatures.

Be praised, my Lord,
for our sister water,
useful and humble,
precious and chaste.